MCGRAW

We love you! Remember
your goals
         Love
            mom

PRIESTHOOD:
SANCTIFYING THE SAINTS

PRIESTHOOD:
SANCTIFYING THE SAINTS

A. HAROLD GOODMAN

Library of Congress
Card Catalog Number 93-70126

ISBN: 1-55517-101-X

Distributed by:

CFI
Cedar Fort, Incorporated
925 North Main, Springville, UT 84663   801-489-4084

Cover Design by Lyle Mortimer
Typeset by Brian Carter

Lithographed in the United States of America

DEDICATION

With deep love, respect and appreciation, this book is dedicated to my eternal companion Naomi and our forever family: Steven, Gordon, Karen, their companions, Grand ones and our parents. They all have completely supported my forty-five years of Church leadership, which have been the foundation for this publication.

Dedicated Priesthood Leaders...

Emulating Inspirational Leadership Qualities...

Honoring Callings from the Lord...

Possessing Sensitive Feelings for Others...

Understanding Effective Leadership...

Implementing Priesthood Programs...

Established Purposes, Goals and Responsibilities...

...Will Perfect and Sanctify the Saints.

TABLE OF CONTENTS

LIST OF ILLUSTRATIONS

PREFACE

What a blessed privilege and responsibility dedicated priesthood leaders have to proclaim the gospel; of Jesus; Christ;, perfect the Saints and redeem the dead. All less active; Church; members, deep down in their souls, seek the support they know the gospel; gives; each nonmember will have eternal joy for having embraced the gospel; and converted souls in the spirit world anxiously plead as they wait to receive God's sacred ordinances. Many blessing are promised the righteous, valiant and effective vessels of the Lord who provide solace to these souls. Power in the priesthood will come from being submissive to our Master's call.

> Therefore, sanctify yourselves that your minds become single to God, and the days will come that you shall see him; for he will unveil his face unto you, and it shall be in his own time, and in his own way, and according to his own will (D&C 88:68).

CHAPTER I

DEDICATED PRIESTHOOD LEADERS...

The Importance of Each Member
The Dignity of the Individual
The Concept of Service
The Spirit of Discernment
Faithful Priesthood Leadership
Sanctification

DEDICATED
PRIESTHOOD LEADERS...

The membership of the Church of Jesus Christ of Latter-day Saints serves as leaders and teachers in wards, branches, stakes, districts and missions throughout the world. The beauty of this plan, in which members serve members, is that it not only gives time, talents and energy to the Church but helps build the potential of each individual who serves in building up the Lord's kingdom. This service contributes to increasing the levels of spirituality and dedication of each member.

The Spirit of the Lord is constantly inspiring all men and women who live on this earth. This is the spirit of truth, the light of the world and has been present since the time of Adam and throughout all generations of time. Each member of the Church who embraces the gospel receives the Holy Ghost by the power of the priesthood and in the name of the Lord Jesus Christ. When a person receives the Holy Ghost, he receives gifts and revelations far beyond the Light of Christ given to all men. The manner whereby the Holy Ghost may aid a member of the Savior's church depends upon that individual's faith, righteousness and desires. The assistance of the Holy Ghost cannot be obtained without living for it. Therefore, service within the Church is essential for spirituality.

Because effective leadership and quality teaching play such a predominant role in the success of the Church and the lives of each member, it is essential for leaders to seek all the insight, inspiration and experience possible. Skills and understandings of leadership will be enhanced when individuals cultivate the power of the priesthood and the Spirit of the Holy Ghost.

THE IMPORTANCE OF EACH MEMBER

The priesthood is given to man that he may receive exaltation and help others gain the same immortal blessings. Spiritual growth through the priesthood is among the most rewarding experiences in mortality; all should strive to cultivate their priesthood power.

Every ward and branch has Church members who are less active or partially active. These Saints are as important to our Heavenly Father as are completely active members. Often less active members are neglected and not made to feel important. The fact that a member has a problem which acts as a magnet pulling him or her away from activity does not excuse the priesthood leadership from its responsibility to these important people. On the contrary, a more diligent effort with greater vision must be exerted. All people need to feel wanted, and all have a burning desire to be drawn into the inner circle of friendship, even though their behavior may not at all times reflect this craving and, instead, may often betray these inner feelings. If inactivity has resulted from justification or rationalization, the member may be more resistant to reactivation.

The major responsibility for initiating a friendshipping program rests primarily with the bishopric, priesthood executive committee, ward council and priesthood quorum leadership. Each member of the bishopric and each quorum leader should be assigned a number of the less active members and then design a program with the home teachers and auxiliary leaders that will bring about full fellowship. Some thoughtful, inspired ward or stake calling needs to be given to every member. Any type of participation should be encouraged—even nonmembers may sing in ward choirs. Too often the most active Saints hold several positions, while those needing the most attention are neglected. With proper planning, implementing and evaluating and with direction by the Spirit of the Holy Ghost, every soul can be reached. Indeed, our Heavenly Father deeply loves each of His children. When the complete ward, or branch, becomes consumed in a caring kind of friendshipping, it is almost overwhelming what can be achieved and how everyone will be blessed.

A dedicated and inspired home teaching program can be an ideal catalyst for permanently bringing souls back into God's fold. Sometimes it may take months and even years to be completely successful, but rest assured it is worth every effort, and blessings will pour out from heaven upon all those involved in the reactivation process. If, after a period of time, home teachers are not proving successful with their families, reassignments are in order. Somewhere in the ward or branch is someone with the love, perception, personality, spirit and concern necessary to activate these souls far beyond expectation. Through humble prayer and fasting, a solution to each person's inactivity will be found. Alma the prophet provided an example for each of us when he said:

> Behold, O Lord, their souls are precious, and many of them are our brethren; therefore, give unto us, O Lord, power and wisdom that we may bring these, our brethren, again unto thee. (Alma 31:35)

Brother Jones was a less active member who continually denied home teachers permission to enter his home. This pattern continued for many years. Finally, a good brother of the ward assigned to Brother Jones was inspired to make whatever sacrifices and efforts necessary to friendship this man. Day after day and night after night, his efforts were in vain because Brother Jones either was not home or would not answer the door. After considerable fasting and praying, the home teacher was inspired to visit at four in the morning. He waited outside the home until five o'clock, when a light in the upstairs apartment went on. He then climbed the stairs and, with courage, knocked on the front door. Brother Jones opened the door and when he could see the intense desire and concern of his home teacher, invited him into the apartment. Once inside, the home teacher said, "Brother Jones, I have been assigned as your home teacher."

Brother Jones then replied, "Any person that is this interested in me is welcome in my home."

With proper friendshipping, love and attention, this less active brother was soon brought back into full activity in the Church and, within a short period of time, was holding major roles of responsibility in the ward.

In the Book of Mormon we read:

> Now they were desirous that salvation should be declared to every creature, for they could not bear that any human soul should perish; yea, even the very thoughts that any soul should endure endless torment did cause them to quake and tremble (Mosiah 28:3).

Another convincing passage reads:

> For I pray continually for them by day, and mine eyes water my pillow by night, because of them; and I cry unto my God in faith, and I know that he will hear my cry (2 Nephi 33:3).

THE DIGNITY OF THE INDIVIDUAL

When man was created to be a living soul with a mortal body, he was meant to have dignity and respect. No ward or branch member should ever be embarrassed or made to feel as if he or she is not accepted. Satan will do everything in his power to make people feel unwanted and drive them to inactivity. Often, less active members use the weaknesses of active Saints, unfortunate experiences or misconceptions of the gospel as excuses for their inactivity. The priesthood leadership will have to strive, search and pray continually for ways to bring dignity into the lives of all ward and branch members. Again, those who are the least active will need the most attention. Every person has worth, talent and capabilities; consequently, these good qualities need to be used as the source for activity and spiritual development. Once a person feels he is wanted and needed, his own self-respect is enhanced, his spirit is rekindled and his activity will develop naturally. This short life on earth is an extremely important stage of man's eternal development. The Lord has said, "For behold, this is my work and glory—to bring to pass the immortality and eternal life of man" (Moses 1:39).

THE CONCEPT OF SERVICE

Some of the most exciting experiences in this life come
about through pure service to others. Priesthood leaders
must be completely immersed in service to others without
expecting benefits in return. A dedicated and devoted ward
member gives of himself to the full ward membership
without unrighteous aspirations to honor, glory, callings,
recognition or rewards. When our Heavenly Father's second
great commandment is fulfilled, an unfeigned love, both
indescribable and uncontainable, will reign as we love our
neighbors as ourselves. (Matthew 19:19) There is greater
joy in helping others to be more successful than is found in
one's own success. A good leader can rejoice in the success
of his peers, and he will be blessed and sanctified for his
rejoicing. Our Savior has said, "For whoso is faithful unto
obtaining these two priesthoods of which I have spoken, and
the magnifying their calling, are sanctified by the Spirit unto
the renewing of their bodies. They become the sons of
Moses and of Aaron and the seed of Abraham, and the
church and kingdom, and the elect of God." (D&C 84:33-
34)

A mission president met a couple as they arrived at the
airport to begin their mission. A grand spirit emanated from
this dedicated couple as the mission president thanked them

for the sacrifices they were making to serve the Lord. Without hesitation, the elder said, "Oh no, president. It is never a sacrifice to serve the Lord. Maybe an inconvenience, but never a sacrifice." Jesus has said, "...no man, having put his hand to the plough, and looking back, is fit for the kingdom of God" (Luke 9:62). Another passage reiterates: "...if you should serve him with all your whole souls yet ye would be unprofitable servants" (Mosiah 2:21).

In the Doctrine and Covenants the Lord says:

> Therefore, O ye that embark in the service of God, see that ye serve him with all your heart, might, mind and strength, that ye may stand blameless before God at the last day (D&C 4:2).

This concept of service requires going beyond the minimal duties of a calling, and this effort is merely the beginning if results are to be maximum. Minimal effort will bring only minimal results. No home teacher should rest until all families under his jurisdiction are completely active and working toward immortality and eternal life with temple sealings. A genuine servant does no fault finding, backbiting, criticizing or negative thinking, anything that would be detrimental to the service being rendered. Satan thoroughly relishes these tools, along with discouragement, to thwart the work of our Heavenly Father. Our Lord and Master has said, "Ye are the light of the world. A city that is set on a hill cannot be hid. Neither do men light a candle, and put it under a bushel, but on a candlestick; and it giveth light unto all that are in the house. Let your light so shine before men, that they may see your good works and glorify your Father which is in Heaven." (Matthew 5:14-16)

The miracle of serving gives us the promise of Jesus, that by losing ourselves we find ourselves. President David O. McKay said, "Joy comes through creation; sorrow through destruction" (*Rules for Living, #2*). Joy springs out of selflessness and service.

There is security in spirituality, and service enhances spirituality. Elder Mark E. Petersen stated:

> The thing which is of most worth unto us is to be in the service of the Lord. This means that we must not be blinded by the glitter of gold or the allurement of position or pleasure or even the false excitement of sin. We must open our eyes to the fact that to serve God is the greatest career in the world (Conference Report, Oct. 1973, pp. 140-144).

Always remember, the Lord shapes the back to fulfill the calling.

THE SPIRIT OF DISCERNMENT

To all men in some degree and to faithful Saints in particular is given the spirit, gift and power of discernment. This power is conferred upon people by the operations of the Light of Christ. In addition, the faithful Saints receive discerning power through revelation from our Heavenly Father by the Spirit of the Holy Ghost.

In its most important aspect, discernment is used to distinguish between good and evil, between the righteous and the wicked, between the false or evil spirits and those spirits who truly manifest the things of God. In its fullest manifestation, the gift of the discerning of spirits is poured out upon presiding officials in God's kingdom; it is given to them to discern all gifts and all spirits, lest any come among the Saints and practice deception.

There is no perfect operation of the power of discernment without revelation. Therefore, "open ye your ears and hearken to the voice of the Lord your God,...a discerner of the thoughts and intents of the heart" (D&C 33:1). Where the Saints are concerned—because they have received the right to the constant companionship of the Holy Ghost—the Lord expects them to discern not only between the righteous and the wicked, but between false and true philosophies, educational theories, science's political concepts, and social schemes. Unfortunately, in many instances, even good men hearken to "the tradition of their fathers" and rely on the learning of the world rather than the revelations of the Lord so that they do not enjoy the full guidance of the spirit of discernment. (D&C 93:39)

There is no reason that members of the Church should not have a thorough understanding of the principles of the gospel, of the order of the Church, and the government of the Church. None need be led astray by any false wind of doctrine or misleading notion that prevails among the children of men. If members of the Church are firmly grounded in the faith and built upon the rock, they will know the truth—the truth which will make them free. Do not doubt there is a lying and deceiving spirit abroad in the land.

If one understands the Articles of Faith and sacred covenants of the Church, and if one will read the scriptures and become familiar with those principles recorded in revelations from the Lord, it will not be necessary to ask questions regarding the authenticity of any purported revelation, vision or manifestation that proceeds out of darkness, concocted in some corner and surreptitiously presented (instead of through proper channels of the Church).

It should be understood that these two influences, good and evil, are manifest in the world through the ministrations of actual spirit personages from the unseen world. Satan's power and influence are exercised through the host of evil spirits who do his bidding and who have power, according to existing laws, to impress their wills upon the minds of receptive mortals. On the other hand, much of the power and influence of Deity is exercised by and manifest through the Holy Ghost, who gives revelation and guidance as the Lord's purposes require. In general, the more righteous and saintly a person becomes, the easier it will be for him to receive communications from heavenly sources; and the more evil and corrupt he is, the easier it will be for evil spirits to deeply implant their nefarious schemes in his mind and heart.

A problem that most people have is knowing what is of God and what is not. The gift of discernment, that is the discerning of spirits, is itself one of the gifts of the spirit that come from God.

It is impossible to hide a bad spirit from the eyes of those who are faithful, because this bad spirit will show itself in speaking, in writing and in all other conduct. It is also a vain attempt to make great pretenses, because the heart is not right. God will expose false exhortations to the faithful. True discernment cannot come to a person who is so self-centered that he gives no thought to others.

FAITHFUL PRIESTHOOD LEADERSHIP

If one were to ask which work is of the greatest worth, the answer would have to be that of bringing souls unto Christ. The Savior has said, "And now, behold, I say unto you, that the thing which will be of the most worth unto you will be to declare repentance unto this people, that you may bring souls unto me, that you may rest with them in the kingdom of my Father" (D&C 15:6). Consequently, to proclaim the gospel of Jesus Christ, to perfect the living and redeem the dead, as commanded by our living prophets, should be clear goals for everyone. Blessings generally do not come from simply being ordained or set apart, but as a result of discharging duties and magnifying callings. A faithful priesthood leader has the promises of sanctification by the Spirit fulfilled in the renewing of the body and in being named among the elect of God. To properly magnify a calling, one must live by every word that proceeds from the mouth of the Lord. Such living requires both knowledge of the gospel and dedicated service.

Elder Mark E. Petersen said, on this subject:

> We all have our own free agency, it is true. We have the right to accept or reject, and that is also true. This is a free country, and I hope it will always remain so. But I would like to make myself clear on this point: When we accept an

assignment in the Church, we accept the responsibility of carrying on the duties and program that pertain to that position. It is not optional with us as to whether we will carry on the program related to this appointment. It is optional whether we accept the position in the first place. For example, if we are called to be bishop or counselor or president, it is optional with us whether we accept the call or not. A man does not have to become a bishop or a counselor or president if he doesn't want to. He has his free agency and may reject the offer. But, if he accepts the position, he then accepts the responsibilities, the duties, and the programs that pertain to that appointment. Therefore, he is obliged as long as he holds the position, to carry on the programs that pertain to that position (England London Mission Conference, 1984).

President Joseph Fielding Smith gave us this warning:

If we do not use the talents given us now and do not exercise the responsibility we have received in this life, then we will not be prepared or worthy to exercise authority and have responsibility there [in the next life].

Our Savior said:

Verily, verily, I say unto you, I will impart unto you of my Spirit, which will enlighten your mind which shall fill your soul with joy; and then shall ye know, or by this shall you know, all things whatsoever you desire of me, which are pertaining unto things of righteousness, in faith believing in me that you shall receive. (D&C 11:13-14)

SANCTIFICATION

Each priesthood leader should constantly be concerned with the sanctification, both spiritual and temporal, of the Saints over whom he presides.

Spiritual sanctification is a process whereby all become pure from sin, more holy and sacred, more committed to keeping God's commandments, more effective vessels in building His kingdom, more able to develop stronger testimonies of the gospel of Jesus Christ, and more able to improve in all matters pertaining to His spirit and eternal life.

Temporal sanctification refers to those aspects of mortal life that can enhance one's effectiveness as a vessel of the Lord. These have to do with success in relationships with people, health and physical condition, wise and effective use of time, constructive attitudes and desires, physical and moral cleanliness, financial stability, success in schooling and careers, and success in the home as patriarchs, fathers, mothers, husbands, wives and children.

CHAPTER II

EMULATING INSPIRATIONAL LEADERSHIP QUALITIES...

Humble and Obedient

Righteous and Pure in Heart

Courageous and Seeking Kingdom of God

Unselfish and Exemplary

Sincere and Repentant

Faithful and Respectful of Parents and Church

Clothed in the Whole Armor of God

EMULATING INSPIRATIONAL LEADERSHIP QUALITIES...

Effective priesthood leaders possess many spiritual qualities that will enhance their success as leaders throughout eternity. Although it may be impossible to possess all of the following qualities to the maximum degree, everyone should possess *some* degree of each of these enduring traits. In general, great leaders are great simplifiers and reducers. One must have the insightful capacity to cut through differences of opinion, buffeting, doubt, debate and pessimism to offer a true solution *everyone* can understand, believe and remember. Even though our Heavenly Father expects to be called upon for inspiration and wisdom, He expects much to come from the priesthood leader himself. The leader should appeal to the Spirit to stir the souls of the Saints yet must lunge forward with all the vigor and capacity he possesses in order to be most successful. If he consistently concentrates on the basic mission of the Church to proclaim the gospel, perfect the Saints and redeem the dead, there will be focus and direction in all that he does.

Our Lord and Master has said:

> And no one can assist in this work except he shall be
> humble and full of love, having faith, hope and charity,

being temperate in all things, whatsoever shall be entrusted to his care (D&C 12:8).

The following traits will assist leaders in preparing the way for the spirit of our Heavenly Father to assist them in developing leadership ability.

HUMBLE AND OBEDIENT

To receive the spirit of our Heavenly Father, an effective leader must completely submit himself to God's will. If we can become humble, He will lift us up. We can become so involved with daily activities, anxieties, schedules and anticipated successes that humility, faith and even the purification and sanctification of the heart are forgotten. Many times, too much success can lead one away from humility. All of the Lord's prophets in the Old Testament possessed humility. Men like Elijah, Samuel the Lamanite, Daniel, Nephi, and President Benson today exemplify this necessary yet rewarding quality. Perhaps when a person is the most humble he becomes the most obedient. "...God resisteth the proud, but giveth grace unto the humble.... Humble yourselves in the sight of the Lord, and He shall lift you up." (James 4:6, 10) The Lord has said, "I am bound when ye do what I say; but when ye do not what I say, ye have no promise" (D&C 82:10).

With humility, a priesthood leader is prepared to be more obedient, valiant and faithful. A good leader obeys the Lord's prophets. "Surely the Lord God will do nothing, but he revealeth his secret unto his servants the prophets" (Amos 3:7).

RIGHTEOUS AND PURE IN HEART

To be guided and prompted by the Spirit is essential to good leadership. If we are to effectively lead in Christ's church, we must know what the Savior desires. This is the Lord's church, not man's; consequently, anything not of the Lord must be removed in order for us to serve righteously. President David O. McKay stated, "Give heed to God's messages through inspiration. If self-indulgence, jealousy, avarice or worry have deadened your response, pray to the Lord to wipe out this impediment." (*Rules for Living, #9*) A good leader always perseveres in doing what is right, staying away from evil and doing the Lord's will. Seek the Lord in righteousness and the Lord will guide you. "Ask and it shall be given unto you; seek, and ye shall find; knock, and it shall be opened unto you. For everyone that asketh receiveth; and he that seeketh, findeth; and to him that knocketh, it shall be opened." (3 Nephi 14:7-8) We shall be blessed if we have pure hearts and are righteous.

COURAGEOUS AND
SEEKING THE KINGDOM OF GOD

A good leader has the courage to do and say what is right. This may not always be easy to do, particularly when others are not in tune with the Lord's will. It is absolutely essential to truly effective leadership to learn about Christ's teachings and properly live them. "And thou shalt do that which is right and good in the sight of the Lord: that it may be well with thee." (Deuteronomy 6:18).

Often the right idea or correct principle may not be the easiest. But a good leader will be as fearless as Abinadi, fearing not the reproach of men nor their reviling. "Have not I commanded thee? Be strong and of a good courage; be not afraid, neither be thou dismayed: for the Lord thy God is with thee withersoever thou goest." (Joshua 1:9) As a leader is confronted with stability and change, he will learn there is a time to set sail and a time to stay in port. Only in seeking the kingdom of God will the proper direction for any activity, project or principle be found.

UNSELFISH AND EXEMPLARY

Anything of eternal value will be found in the gospel of Jesus Christ, while those things of no value will pass away with all temporal things. When we die, what we *have* goes to another, but what we *are* will be ours forever. So, we should unselfishly and freely give of ourselves with every opportunity. Our Heavenly Father loves a cheerful giver. A grateful heart is a lubricant in life, whereas an ungrateful heart is a friction in life, wasting life, power and energy. An unselfish leader cultivates harmony, unanimity, agreement and joy through his sacrificial service. A selfish leader, on the other hand, creates resistance, conflict, disagreement and sorrow with his counterproductive work.

As leaders, in addition to asking for wisdom and courage, we should pray for kind hearts. "Every man according as he purposeth in his heart, so let him give; not grudgingly, or of necessity; for God loveth a cheerful giver" (II Corinthians 9:7).

SINCERE AND REPENTANT

Alma, the courageous missionary, encouraged us not to procrastinate. He said, "...if we do not improve our time while in this life, then cometh the night of darkness wherein there can be no labor performed" (Alma 35.33). An example of one who suffered the effects of procrastination is Sherem, who repented too late (Jacob 7). A good leader understands the importance of sincerity, repentance and administering to the sacred ordinances of the priesthood. For "without the ordinances thereof, and the authority of the priesthood, the power of godliness is not made manifest unto men in the flesh" (D&C 84:21).

There are many members who do not understand the miraculous power of repentance. Many do not understand the principle of repentance or desire its effect in their lives. These individuals often feel no hope, only despair. However, "...the Lord is merciful unto all who will, in the sincerity of their hearts, call upon his holy name" (Helaman 3:27). No Church member should be deprived of the marvelous blessing of repentance, and priesthood leaders have the responsibility of being sincere and repentant models worth emulating.

FAITHFUL AND RESPECTFUL
OF PARENTS AND CHURCH

What a marvelous promise to know that we shall inherit eternal life, if we are but faithful and endure (D&C 50:5). As leaders, we must be patient with ourselves and with those we serve. If we are loyal to the Church and our families, we will be blessed. The ultimate purpose of mortality is to create eternal family units and perfect the lives of each member of those families. With these ultimate goals in mind, we must catch the vision of the great power we possess in this life, the miraculous creative ability that can bring us eternal joy and godliness through the gospel of Jesus Christ. "And he shall plant in the hearts of the children the promises made to the fathers, and the hearts of the children shall turn to their father" (D&C 2:2).

A successful priesthood leader must not only have all of these qualities but must understand that testimony building, spiritual strength, desire to live the commandments and perfect the lives of the Saints must all occur within the individual. There must be an eternal desire that compels righteousness and spirituality. These individual qualities cannot be imposed upon a person. The door to the human heart can only be opened from within.

William Holman Hunt, great English artist of the Pre-Raphaelite school, painted a garden scene which was hung in the Royal Academy in London. The painting, appropriately called "The Light of the World," shows the Master standing in a garden at night, holding a lantern as he knocks on a door.

A critic examined the painting, turned to Mr. Hunt and said, "Lovely painting, Mr. Hunt, but you've forgotten something. That door upon which the Master is knocking...is it never to be opened? You've forgotten to put a knob on the door."

Mr. Hunt smiled with great understanding. "My friend, that door on which the Master is knocking is not just an ordinary door. It is the door to the human heart. It needs no knob, for it can only be opened from within."

CLOTHED IN THE WHOLE ARMOR OF GOD

As we consider the exemplary life of an effective priesthood leader, the apostle Paul, we are always inspired by his words and deeds. Perhaps to even better prepare ourselves for the mighty reality of spiritual and temporal sanctification, we should put upon ourselves the "whole armour of God." Paul said,

> Be strong in the Lord, and in the power of his might. Put on the whole armour of God, that ye may be able to stand against the wiles of the devil. For we wrestle not against flesh and blood, but against principalities, against the rulers of darkness of this world, against spiritual wickedness in high places. Wherefore take unto you the whole armour of God, that ye may be able to withstand in the evil day, and having done all to stand. (Ephesians 6:10-13)

Our common enemy often cannot be perceived by the bodily senses. So Paul used metaphors when he described each of us as a warrior, clothed in the armor necessary to protect our most vulnerable parts, those that Satan and his spy system know so well. More specifically, Paul said, "Stand therefore, having your loins girt about with truth, and having on the breastplate of righteousness; and your feet shod with the preparation of the gospel of peace...And take the helmet of salvation...." (Ephesians 6:14, 17)

What follows are brief summaries of the function and meaning of the four protective articles referred to in this scripture.

A girdle about the loins

A girdle worn in this way protects the area between the ribs and hips, including all the vital generative organs. A person whose loins are symbolically "girt about with truth" has characteristics of virtue, moral purity, vital strength and cleanliness, and is entitled to the companionship of the Lord's spirit. Such protection provides the wearer with knowledge and strength and glory added upon forever and ever.

A breastplate over the heart

This protective device is made up of righteousness, faith, brotherly kindness, godliness, charity, humility and diligence. The mouth speaks from the heart and determines daily conduct in life. When the heart is shielded, our lives reflect a positive mental attitude, enthusiasm and courage. A person with "a breastplate of righteousness" has the power of convincing men and women through the Lord's spirit.

The feet properly shod

Feet symbolize the journey through life. They give direction, action and speed in implementing priesthood responsibilities. A person whose feet are "shod with the *preparation* of the gospel of peace" has set goals and does not fear, because he is prepared. (Ephesians 6:15)

A helmet upon the head

A helmet protects the head, which houses the intellect. A leader who wears a "helmet of salvation" is empowered with the Christ-like abilities to perceive, ponder and make inspired and informed value judgments. In general, this helmet should accompany leaders as they set priesthood goals and objectives.

Again, from Ephesians, "Above all, taking the shield of faith, wherewith ye shall be able to quench all the fiery darts of the wicked. And take...the sword of the Spirit, which is the word of God." (Ephesians 6:16, 17)

A shield of faith is far more comprehensive than some realize. We must have faith in God our Heavenly Father, in our Lord and Master Jesus Christ, in the gift of the Holy Ghost, in our calling as His vessel, in this restored gospel, in our living prophet today, and in proclaiming, perfecting and redeeming. The sword of the spirit is the power of convincing men of the word of God.

Each priesthood holder should put on the whole armor of God and, with the shield of faith and the sword of the spirit, fulfill his calling to the highest degree of excellence. If he does this, he is promised many eternal rewards and promises:

> And if your eye be single to my glory, your whole bodies shall be filled with light, and there shall be no darkness in you; and that body which is filled with light comprehendeth all things. Therefore, sanctify yourselves that your minds become single to God, and the days will come that you shall see him; for he will unveil his face unto you, and it shall be in his own time, and in his own way, and according to his own will. (D&C 88:67-68)

Also, our Redeemer has said:

> Let thy bowels also be full of charity toward all men, and to the houschold of faith, and let virtue garnish thy thoughts unceasingly; then shall thy confidence wax strong in the presence of God; and the doctrine of the priesthood shall distill upon thy soul as the dew from heaven. The Holy Ghost shall be thy constant companion, and thy scepter an unchanging scepter of righteousness and truth; and thy dominion shall be an everlasting dominion, and without compulsory means it shall flow unto thee forever and ever. (D&C 121:45-46)

CHAPTER III

HONORING CALLINGS
FROM THE LORD...

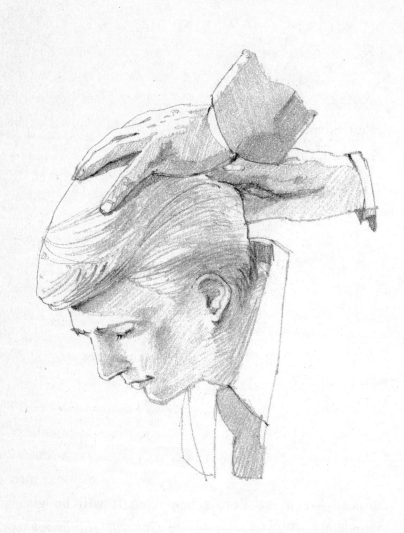

HONORING CALLINGS
FROM THE LORD...

As members and leaders of the Church of Jesus Christ, we have the sacred opportunity and sobering obligation to implement *all* programs of the Church. Our Heavenly Father expects us to do His work effectively and successfully. It is only through the members that this "marvelous work and a wonder" is accomplished; therefore, how successfully God's work goes forth unto all people to completely fill the earth depends on the degree to which each individual accepts his or her responsibility as a disciple of Christ.

The authority for making callings in the Church comes from the Lord. *You* are the only member who can fill the position given you, so it follows that many Saints are depending upon you. Your calling should be considered a high priority; it demands respect, dignity, and honor. Consult often with priesthood leaders to receive as much counsel and instruction as possible. Read all available materials on your calling, organize your time so that you can give sufficient attention to your responsibilities, then earnestly seek the Lord's help, and it will be given abundantly. (Please refer to the *General Handbook of Instructions*, published by the Church of Jesus Christ of Latter-day Saints, Salt Lake City, Utah, 1989.)

"And the sons of Moses and of Aaron shall be filled with the glory of the Lord, upon Mount Zion in the Lord's house, whose sons are ye; And also many whom I have *called* and *sent* forth to build up my church" (D&C 84:32). The priesthood *calls*; it does not *ask* for volunteers.

Every person called to serve in the Church has the right to feel that he or she was called by inspiration. Earnestly seek the Lord's will in all callings and releases, and He will bless you. Extending calls to the Saints is one of the most rewarding aspects of priesthood leadership. In selecting the proper person for a position, know of his or her worthiness, interests, abilities, work and family needs.

In addition to knowing the capabilities of the person under consideration, a priesthood leader should know the requirements of the position to be filled and how the call will benefit the individual and the individual's family. The leader should keep an accurate account of all available talent in the ward and, most important, he should know how to call upon the Lord for inspiration and then confirmation. The priesthood executive committee provides the most appropriate setting in which to discuss ward needs regarding callings.

All information about callings should be kept extremely confidential. Candidates should not be told of a prospective appointment until officially called and, after called, should be cautioned to keep the news a private matter until an official sustaining.

Newly baptized members should be given appropriate callings as quickly as possible. An example of such a calling would be an assistant teacher whose basic responsibility is to help the instructor by reading a scripture or story or by providing other materials that would enhance the class. With such callings, new members are placed in positions where they are making contributions and becoming part of the ward organization from the very beginning. Often this sensitive attention is overlooked. To neglect calling new members of the Church into God's service is to assist them in becoming less active.

EXTENDING THE CALL

Proper interviewing is a significant factor in the success of a calling. There are no rules that require strict conformity in interviewing. In general, priesthood leaders should make a specific appointment for the interview and allow for privacy so that the Spirit of the Lord can reign. To determine worthiness, ask specific questions that are outlined in the *General Handbook of Instructions*..

All callings should be extended with significance and import without apologies. Make details of a call clear and exact, and include all ward and stake obligations. Emphasize the challenges as well as the rewards of the position. Where there are high expectations, performance is high. Conversely, low expectations result in low performance. There should be a definite commitment to the calling when the individual leaves the interview.

The priesthood leader should make sure that membership records for those being called are obtained before calls are extended. Exceptions are made if the individual's former bishop can be contacted. If a child is to be offered a calling, the parents should be consulted before formally extending the call. Also, as a courtesy, a husband should be contacted before extending a call to his wife.

"Verily I say unto you, behold how great is your calling. Cleanse your hearts and your garments, lest the blood of this generation be required at your hands" (D&C 112:33).

"Therefore, let every man stand in his own office, and labor in his own calling; and let not the head say unto the feet it hath no need of the feet; for without the feet how shall the body be able to stand?" (D&C 84:109).

In reviewing personnel and program needs of a ward, stake or organization, develop a program that would be comprehensive and effective. When seeking the proper person for each position, earnestly call upon the Lord for inspiration. After calling upon Him, listen! Avoid giving too many callings to those who always seem qualified. Bring all ward membership into callings of some kind and draw the circle of activity large enough to include everyone. Everyone needs to be needed and wanted. Help members feel that they are making contributions to the Church.

Priesthood "calling" is the order of the Church; "asking" for volunteers is not. When organizations such as the priesthood executive committee, ward choir, and the youth program are in need of help, the procedure is to call, not ask for those willing to volunteer. As previously stated, the pattern is clear; for the Lord has said, "...also many whom I have *called* and sent forth to build up my church" (D&C 84:32, emphasis added).

In one particular ward, more than a third of the membership was completely less active. The inspired bishop, in meeting with his counselors, decided to review the distribution of callings in the ward. He found that many of the active ward members were carrying three and four callings each. After careful review, he reduced these callings to one or two. A list of less active members was made and then divided among the three members of the bishopric. Each bishopric member used his share of the list as a reservoir for all positions that needed filling. The remarkable result was that most of these less active members accepted the callings extended and thus became activated, and the ward had almost total participation by its membership.

Listen to the promptings of the Holy Spirit and you will be guided with understanding, ability, insight and vision far beyond your expectations. The ultimate goal is to have every ward member receive all the sacred ordinances of the Lord's holy temple, creating eternal families units which keep His covenants and work toward eternal godliness. To accomplish this goal requires righteous activity in the Church and home from the beginning of life in mortality until passing on to the spirit world. The success of every father will be determined primarily by the spiritual influence he had on his family throughout mortality. So, priesthood leader, make your ward members' callings ones that will strengthen the family and home at all times. This is what our Heavenly Father would desire.

The officer extending the call should give the member being called the names of those with whom he or she will be working. He should also recommend handbooks, manuals and other available materials; discuss required meetings; and, in general, define the responsibilities of the calling while determining the worthiness of the individual to serve. Last, he should keep a record of all appointments and releases and then submit it to the proper authority.

SUSTAINING AND SETTING APART

Generally, those called to Church positions are sustained by a vote of the ward or stake membership concerned. It is appropriate to ask the person or group to stand when presented and remain standing until after the sustaining vote. Voting is done by raising the right hand. During sustainings, it is important for members to remember the *person* being sustained rather than the action of the presiding authority. An opposing vote should be made only when an unresolved worthiness problem or transgression is known of and *never* because of personal feelings or disagreements. Reasons for this dissenting vote should be heard in private by the priesthood leadership.

All stake priesthood and auxiliary officers and all ward officers and teachers are to be set apart. (Please see the *General Handbook of Instructions* for definitive instruction.) Home teachers and visiting teachers are not set apart. Again, accurate records should be kept of all sustainings and releases.

EXTENDING THE RELEASE

The same quality attention offered in extending call should be given in the release, including an interview and sustaining vote of appreciation by the organization concerned. Often the release is treated as insignificant, which is not only unfortunate but demeaning to the person who has willingly served. An expression of gratitude indicates a heightened perception of understanding. Bad feelings, even inactivity, may result from an improper release.

> "For it is required of the Lord, at the hand of every steward, to render an account of his stewardship, both in time and in eternity. For he who is faithful and wise in time is accounted worthy to inherit the mansions prepared for him of my Father." (D&C 72:3-4)

SACRED STEWARDSHIP

Irrespective of the call, service is a sacred stewardship in the kingdom of God. Time, talents, property, families, callings—all of these He has entrusted as part of one's individual stewardship.

And as they heard these things, he added and spake a parable, because he was nigh to Jerusalem, and because they thought that the kingdom of God should immediately appear.

He said therefore, A certain nobleman went into a far country to receive for himself a kingdom, and to return.

And he called his ten servants, and delivered them ten pounds, and said unto them, Occupy till I come.

But his citizens hated him, and sent a message after him, saying, We will not have this man to reign over us. And it came to pass, that when he was returned, having received the kingdom, then he commanded these servants to be called unto him, to whom he had given the money, that he might know how much every man had gained by trading.

Then came the first, saying, Lord, thy pound hath gained ten pounds.

And he said unto him, Well, thou good servant: because thou hast been faithful in a very little, have thou authority over ten cities.

And the second came, saying, Lord, thy pound hath gained five pounds.

And he said likewise to him, Be thou also over five cities. And another came, saying, Lord, behold, here is thy pound, which I have kept laid up in a napkin:

For I feared thee, because thou art an austere man: thou takest up that thou layedst not down, and reapest that thou didst not sow.

And he saith unto him, Out of thine own mouth will I judge thee, thou wicked servant. Thou knewest that I was an austere man, taking up that I laid not down, and reaping that I did not sow:

Wherefore then gavest not thou my money into the bank, that at my coming I might have required mine own with usury?

And he said unto them that stood by, Take from him the pound, and give it to him that hath ten pounds.

(And they said unto him, Lord, he hath ten pounds.)

For I say unto you, That unto every one which hath shall be given; and from him that hath not, even that he hath shall be taken away from him." (Luke 19:11-26)

The following worksheets provide important information regarding the calls themselves. These should be completed as indicated and given to the appropriate people (also indicated). Leaders may find these worksheets helpful in evaluating stewardship during interviews. A principle to remember is that performance improves when measured, but performance improves remarkably when measured *and* reported.

WHAT IS EXPECTED

Name:
Church position:

Brief description of the calling:

Meetings to attend:
　Sacrament meeting weekly
　Priesthood meeting weekly (male members)
　Stake conferences
　Your organization's planning and leadership meetings

(To be filled out by the individual requesting the position be filled.
The information is intended to be used by the person making the call
to explain general responsibilities of the position.)

WHAT IS EXPECTED

Considerations and requirements of the calling:

(To be filled out by the immediate priesthood leader after the position has been accepted. The information should detail considerations and requirements necessary for performing well in the calling.)

REPORTING YOUR STEWARDSHIP

Your name:
Church position:

Evaluate your progress in striving to meet the goals you set when first called.

Accomplishments:

Failures:

New short-range goals:

(To be filled out and submitted quarterly to the immediate supervisor, who should conduct a stewardship interview.)

THE PRINCIPLE OF WORK

From a crucible of work emerges the hard core of character. The crucible serves as a conversion laboratory. Our work determines the type of life we are building forever. Consider the character President Spencer W. Kimball established for himself with a dedication to hard work. It has been said that when the prophet's physician told him to slow down and not go so fast, President Kimball replied, "Your job is, Brother Wilkinson, to keep me going at the pace I am going to go!"

A sluggish farmer went to his doctor for help. The doctor told him that he was burning his candle at both ends. The farmer replied: "I knew that before I came here. What I want from you is more wax!"

The family or career should certainly not be neglected as you serve in the Church. But with a convincing desire to serve our Lord and Master, and with His spirit, we will be blessed with more effective relationships within our families and with more successful careers, while being more fruitful vessels of the Lord.

Desire is the ingredient that makes the difference between a saved soul and an exalted being. As we sow, so also shall we reap. When you sow an action you reap a habit; when you sow a habit you reap a character; when you sow a character you reap a destiny. The destiny for each of us is exaltation. (Adapted from a poem by E.D. Boardman that was quoted by David O. McKay, in Conference Report, Spring 1962, p. 7.)

The mind works like a garden:

1. To have a garden, you must plant seed into soil.

2. If you plant corn, you won't get tomatoes—you will raise corn.

3. You don't plant a seed to raise one kernel of corn. You plant a seed to raise *hundreds* of kernels.

4. Between planting and harvest there is much work and tremendous increase.

Likewise:

1. Every thought that goes into your mind has an effect, good or bad.

2. Plant negative thoughts, reap negative thoughts; plant positive thoughts, reap positive thoughts.

3. Plant a negative thought and reap many negative thoughts. Plant a positive thought and reap many positive thoughts.

4. Every effort made in producing good thoughts is beneficial.

Our future destiny as priesthood leaders forever will be determined in large measure by:

- how we honor the priesthood.
- how we honor the leaders of our wards and stakes.
- how we honor our living prophet.
- how we honor the callings given us in the Church.
- how we keep the commandments that bring eternal glory.
- the righteous desires we develop in our lives.
- the example we are to others and the influence for good that we become.
- the faith we build in our Lord and Master Jesus Christ.

Verily, verily, I say unto you, even as you desire of me so it shall be done unto you; and, if you desire, you shall be the means of doing much good in this generation. (D&C 11:8)

CHAPTER IV

POSSESSING SENSITIVE
FEELINGS FOR OTHERS...

Wise Delegation

Motivational Leadership

POSSESSING SENSITIVE
FEELINGS FOR OTHERS...

A priesthood leader may know and understand his calling thoroughly but often may not realize the distinct humanizing skills that are needed in motivating and inspiring people. To be a catalyst for good in the lives of people requires perception, sensitivity and concern for the attitudes, feelings and needs of others. People react and respond the way they do because of reasons, whether known or unknown. Each person is different and should be treated according to his or her experiences, background and understandings. The human being is the most marvelous of all creations and, consequently, the most complex. Ideas or feelings that relate to one person may not relate to another because the verbal symbolism used will have significantly different meanings for both. What a person sees or how a person feels may have a stronger influence on that person's behavior than we know.

The following delegation principles and motivational leadership concepts will help each priesthood leader become more effective in his own stewardship.

WISE DELEGATION

The greatest teacher who ever lived, our Savior, has given us inspirational and promising lessons on effective leadership. Delegating wisely is an important process in the success of a program and improvement of the Saints. The following ideas may be helpful in giving further insight and understanding to proper delegation.

1. The organization Jesus established was structural in its framework of delegated authority.

2. Jesus did not make assignments or callings sound easy, but He *did* made them sound exciting, challenging and rewarding.

3. Jesus let those called know their duties in explicit detail.

4. Jesus placed complete and unquestioning confidence in those to whom He delegated just as His Heavenly Father had done with Him.

5. Jesus gave complete loyalty to those He called and expected their loyalty in return.

6. Jesus expected much from those to whom He delegated responsibility. There was no compromise.

7. Jesus seemed to invite feedback and evaluation from those to whom He gave assignments.

8. Jesus taught that he who leads should follow the progress of those to whom responsibility has been delegated, giving praise and reproof in a spirit of love. If these concepts are used as major guidelines by priesthood leaders, much success will be achieved.

And now, behold, I give unto you a commandment, that when ye are assembled together ye shall instruct and edify each other, that ye may know how to act and direct my church (D&C 43:8).

MOTIVATIONAL LEADERSHIP

There are many humanizing aspects of leadership that would be helpful to every priesthood leader. The following suggestions should be reviewed and then adapted to suit each individual's personality.

1. Priesthood leaders must realize first, last and always that only through other people is it possible for them to succeed.

2. Make it a point to know what your co-workers' interests are and take the trouble to exhibit your own interest in and respect for these interests. Keep in mind each person's habits and hobbies, what he knows and what he believes.

3. In giving explanations or directions, be careful to speak in the language of the Saints whom you are directing.

4. When you help another person, make it easy for him to cancel the hidden obligation. Do not place a person under an obligation he cannot return. By safeguarding another person's pride, you give him a strong incentive to help you in return.

5. One way of building goodwill among co-workers is to request a favor of them, one that you know they will enjoy granting.

6. Every priesthood leader needs to make it a definite part of his personal administrative skills to be able to listen attentively when others speak to him.

7. Perhaps the best way to increase your depth of understanding is by inviting people to talk about their own affairs and problems. Show your interest by your manner of listening.

8. With all sincerity, every priesthood leader must take pains to show he considers his co-workers important.

9. No priesthood leader can ever afford the luxury of allowing himself to think of another person as unimportant or inferior, and certainly he must never belittle the importance of anyone in public.

10. Enthusiasm is developed for the plans of a priesthood leader by inducing co-workers to participate in those plans. If possible, a leader should guide the participation of his co-workers so they may begin by doing something that is easy for them to them to

accomplish yet something they will regard as a real achievement.

11. It is a good practice to draw opposing parties out and listen to what they have to say. A priesthood leader needs to demonstrate that he thoroughly understands the position these parties have taken, even if he cannot agree with them. Often a good strategy is for him to restate an objection with even more emphasis than it was given to him originally.

12. No priesthood leader should permit himself to be drawn into an argument, especially with a person who is relatively uninformed on the issue in question. An argument is nearly always useless and may often be very harmful.

13. When prompt action is desired on a proposed activity, a priesthood leader should present it in a definite form as a concrete proposal or as a clear-cut issue.

14. A good priesthood leader must be accessible. He must make it easy for people with concerns to see him, and he must let it be known he is always ready and glad to listen.

15. Every good priesthood leader must safeguard the self-esteem of his co-workers and the others with whom he works. He must protect them from his own desire to feel superior and important. This desire, whether we realize it or not, is always at work within each of us.

16. A priesthood leader often best exercises his authority when he makes it clear that he considers the principle or policy in question more important than himself.

17. An important function of a good priesthood leader is to serve as a "shock absorber," to protect others so that they may work more effectively. Although a leader absorbs many shocks which concern other people, he must transmit relatively few of them.

18. It is poor practice for a priesthood leader to put someone in an embarrassing position, even if he believes he has good cause to do so.

19. Every successful priesthood leader must be ready and willing to share the limelight with his co-workers and, for their successes, give them adequate credit and praise. Likewise, he must be ready and willing to shoulder at least a portion of the blame for their mistakes, perhaps even more than is his fair portion.

20. In choosing Saints for callings, a good priesthood leader will endeavor to find the person the Lord would want to be selected.

21. The intelligent priesthood leader has learned to disregard his first impressions about people. On the whole, these impressions are likely to be unsound because most people, on occasion of first contact, endeavor to be on guard and strive to make a deliberate favorable impression.

22. No priesthood leader can afford to give the appearance of ignoring even the least of his co-workers. All people need to be noticed.

23. A good priesthood leader is not afraid to show his co-workers that he empathizes with their problems. It is not enough to feel such empathy. The important thing is to let co-workers recognize you care. Remember: "I don't care how much you know until I know how much you care."

24. Most priesthood leaders probably praise their co-workers too little rather than too much. Praise is a powerful method of stimulating interest, loyalty and

better work. When it is given, though, it must always be sincere.

25. An effective priesthood leader must be humble and establish a reputation of modesty. He knows that the credit others give him of their own accord is greater than any credit he may gain by making claims for himself.

26. When co-workers or other people express an honest difference of opinion, a wise priesthood leader does not take it as a personal affront.

27. Every priesthood leader must develop the ability to respect and hold a confidence. He must resist the temptation to impress by repeating a "secret" that has come to him as a result of his position. He must remember that many people are on the alert to profit by his unguarded remarks and that few of them will respect his lack of confidence.

28. When situations develop in which there are tense feelings among people, humor often works to create a pleasing means of relieving tension and drawing people together.

29. A priesthood leader should remember that spirit and emotion are contagious. He should endeavor at all times to be pleasant in his relationships with his co-workers and others.

CHAPTER V

UNDERSTANDING EFFECTIVE LEADERSHIP...

Organizing

Implementing

Evaluating

Committee and Council Leadership

Internal Consistency: Peace and Pride

UNDERSTANDING EFFECTIVE LEADERSHIP...

All things should have definition and direction. In order to effectively shape and implement programs and activities, the leadership must have a clear and unified understanding of purposes, goals and objectives.

One of the first steps in planning is to insure there is a basic understanding between the ward or stake member and the priesthood leader about the responsibilities to be performed. Both parties should participate in making the performance list. A person cannot be completely successful in his performance if the role he envisions is different than the role perceived by the priesthood leader. A good axiom to remember is, "He who does the work should help set the goal." Effective change comes about when the person being called takes a prominent role in establishing procedure and evaluating performance. Such leading questions as "What is going well?" "How can we improve?" and "What can I do to help?" generally open the door for strong participation and involvement.

An important thing to remember about goal setting is that it need not necessarily be approached formally. Formalized approaches often force the objectives of a particular assignment to peripheral aspects. When a person is asked to formally prepare objectives, he thinks in terms of new programs rather than the day-to-day aspects of the position itself. The secret is to determine weaknesses and strengths of a particular program and then effectively achieve the goals that have been set.

Ways of exerting leadership by supporting, assisting and sharing decision-making include:

1. Completely reviewing all manuals, guidebooks and handbooks.

2. Having informal discussions of program improvements.

3. Approaching members by asking insightful questions.

4. Creating a "think-tank" situation where all possible creative ideas may be generated.

5. Preparing a formal list for review.

6. Reviewing other successful programs.

7. Inviting resource people to assist.

8. Presenting ideas in an objective manner for significance ratings and value judgments.

Regardless of the approach used to evoke ideas for improvement, an accurate and detailed record should be kept so that each member involved may have a written report of what has been shared. At times, secretaries may be invited to attend for recording purposes. Other times, listings on a blackboard are sufficient. Avoid use of tape recorders, because this mode can intimidate true expression.

ORGANIZING

Members need to be surrounded with all available resources in order to most effectively attain their goals. Resources may include the meetinghouse library, assistants, handbooks, guidebooks, budget, audio or visual hardware, even space utilization. Each member must come to a realization that his or her priesthood leader will do all within his power to help achieve the objectives that have been established. Suggestions regarding organization and procedure should, again, be mutually prepared. To organize means to have a plan that defines direction and ultimately leads to success.

IMPLEMENTING

In all sincerity, every priesthood leader must take pains to show that he considers his co-workers important. He should remember that emotions are contagious and should endeavor at all times to be good humored and pleasant in his relationships with them. He should be interested in the progress of these members, showing support and never questioning or showing a lack of confidence in them.

The priesthood leader should hold personal priesthood interviews with each member under his jurisdiction. The date of the review should be determined by both. During the review, the leader should write down the progress the member has made. Let it be emphasized again that flexibility in methods and procedures should probably be used at the different levels of administration. Sometimes once-a-month progress reviews are advantageous; sometimes reviews should be held quarterly. The important thing is to develop a system that works for the Saints involved. Whatever works best is the pattern to use.

It is not necessary for a person to have multiple objectives at the beginning of the objective year. Two or three objectives may be adequate, depending on the circumstances. A member may complete an objective early in the year. In this case, he or she will want additional objectives.

Approximately once a year, a confidential visit needs to be held with each leader regarding other goals related to the calling. These are broad objectives or purposes (how the member would make the greatest contribution to the ward or stake). The visit might even relate to the member's family. An important thing to remember is that as the individual improves in any way as a "whole person," he becomes a better member of the Church.

EVALUATING

Leaders themselves are generally the most critical of, and thus render the best value judgments about, their own achievements. It is important for them to realize that there will be an evaluation of their performance. Those in executive positions should establish a policy of flexibility in altering goals when necessary.

A great challenge for any priesthood leader is determining how to make those under his leadership most effective and successful. Individual approaches, such as those mentioned, will indeed assist each member in fulfilling his greatest contribution.

Above all, make certain that everyone feels "part of the Lord's team" and not as if standing on the "outside looking in." Because of the nature of executive leadership, an inner ring will naturally be created. All have the desire to be inside this ring, and all have a great fear of being left outside looking in. This desire is one of the never-ending mainsprings of human concern. A good priesthood leader will express what is expected of each person under his leadership and assist in strengthening each to live up to those expectations. Always be cautious that circles are not drawn to exclude ward members. Draw a large enough circle to bring in all of the ward.

COMMITTEE AND COUNCIL LEADERSHIP

The term "committee work" has a basic connotation of a task force. It is impossible for one person to collect all the data needed in a complex program; consequently, committees and councils are needed for this purpose.

Members involved in implementing decisions should be involved in making those decisions. Because of the complexity and nature of tasks, one or two individuals cannot be expected to perform all of them. The work needs to be parceled out to ward members, not only to get successful contributions, but also to assist all members in becoming part of the team.

The leadership must have an understanding of how committee meetings can be of the best quality. The following is a listing of characteristics members like most about committees and councils that function well:

1. The committee has a defined role. All members understand the main goal and clearly see their individual responsibilities to that end.

2. Meetings are carefully controlled; they start and end on time. Meetings are limited to the time it takes to get the work done, no longer.

3. Committee and council members are sensitive to each other's needs and expressions. Members listen to and respect others' opinions.

4. The atmosphere is informal and relaxed.

5. Priesthood leaders and committee members are thoroughly prepared. Materials are prepared and available.

6. Members are qualified and interested. They want to be a part of the organization. A definite commitment exists.

7. Interruptions are avoided.

8. Accurate minutes or records are kept so that decisions are not lost.

9. Periodically, the council stops and assesses its own performance. Needed improvements are worked out.

10. Council members feel they are given some kind of reward for their efforts. Recognition and appreciation are expressed, making them feel they are really making a contribution.

Almost any organization can substantially improve members' productivity simply by adhering to basic time-control procedures. Always remember that meetings are generally not conducive to creative thinking. Meetings are basically a means of communication. Always strive to have the spirit of our Heavenly Father present. A time-controlled meeting requires that the individual organize his thoughts *before* the meeting starts.

Here are some suggestions which should be observed if a meeting is to be time-controlled:

1. An agenda should be provided for meetings where more than one subject is to be discussed.
    a. List general subjects open for discussion.
    b. Identify specific topics under study by reviewing minutes from the previous meeting.
    c. Discuss topics in detail and determine new ones through open communication between committee members.

2. Committee members should have pre-planned timetables.
    a. Committee members should know when the meeting will commence and when it will end so that they can intelligently plan time for other responsibilities.
    b. People spend time like money. Without limitations, people will spend too much. If you think discussion

of a given point should take about twenty minutes,
budget fifteen minutes and state this budget figure
in the agenda timetable.

   c. Encourage members to "stick to the subject," but in
exercising time control, never go so far as to make
them feel they are being cut short or forced into
making decisions with insufficient facts.

3. People attending a meeting should always be advised
beforehand of the contribution that will be expected
from them.

   a. Committee members should organize their thoughts
and materials before a meeting, using their own
time.

   b. If the agenda does not fully explain an important
subject, supplement the agenda with a
memorandum addressed to those members
responsible for the discussion.

4. Minutes of a meeting should narrate simply the
following:

   a. The principle solutions, ideas or facts considered for
each point on the agenda.

   b. The conclusion reached on each point.

    c. A description of any further action to be taken,
       including *who* is to take action and *when* further
       action is to take place.

All activity should, of course, take place under the influence of the Lord's spirit.

Obviously, evaluation of programs is subjective and complex, at the very least. But the complexity does not remove the responsibility. This challenging evaluation process includes identifying strengths as well as weaknesses. Each person under a leader's direction will be different; consequently, the approach he uses to help each discover where he or she is strong or weak will have to be flexible and insightful. Needless to say, this is such a profound and sacred assignment that complete and reciprocal confidence between the priesthood leader and the member is an absolute necessity. It is best that the member be taught the more correct procedures and principles and then be left to fulfill own stewardship.

CHAPTER VI

IMPLEMENTING PRIESTHOOD PROGRAMS...

Home Teaching

Ward Priesthood Executive Committee

Ward Council

Family Home Evening

Gospel-Oriented Teaching

Traits of a Good Gospel Teacher

Guide for Increasing Spirituality

IMPLEMENTING PRIESTHOOD PROGRAMS...

There are inspired programs that help the leaders of wards and stakes improve the spirituality and activity of ward members. When these programs are defined, understood, and then given direction, everyone receives glorious blessings. On the contrary, if ward leaders neglect such programs as the ward priesthood executive committee; ward council; priesthood quorums; home teaching and visiting teaching; missionary, temple and genealogy work; and the calling of effective gospel teachers, one can predict a ward that will not receive all of the blessings to which it is entitled.

Too often a bishop or quorum leader takes the major burden of a calling and does not share, delegate, or use ward resources, all of which would make him more effective. There was a bishop in a certain ward who felt he should do everything—even make out the tithing receipts. Needless to say, as fine a person as he was, he was ineffective, exhausted, and broken in spirit. There was another bishop who never planned, gave direction, implemented decisions or evaluated activities in the ward. This ward was almost in chaos. If the programs of a ward, quorum, or organization are properly implemented as designed by the Church (and *all* resources identified and mutually used) there should be complete success and joy among members.

HOME TEACHING

Home teaching is the vehicle that implements the goals of the Priesthood Executive Committee. The ultimate purpose of home teaching is to assist in exalting the family—the celestial and eternal unit. Missionary, temple, family history, and welfare programs are carried to homes by way of home teachers. The stewardship of the home teacher can best be expressed in the instructions given by the great prophet Ezekiel:

> Son of Man, I have made thee a watchman unto the house of Israel: therefore hear the word at my mouth, and give them warning from me. When I say unto the wicked, Thou shalt surely die; and thou givest him not warning, nor speakest to warn the wicked from his wicked way, to save his life; the same wicked man shall die in his iniquity; but his blood will I require at thine hand. Yet, if thou warn the wicked and he turn not from his wickedness, nor from his wicked way, he shall die in his iniquity; but thou hast delivered thy soul. (Ezekiel 3:17-19)

This stewardship, having received priesthood keys, is a sacred trust. Literally, ward members' lives are placed in the hands of their home teachers, and an accounting for these individuals will have to be given in the day of the Lord. The bishop has the duty to see that all souls in the confines of his ward become celestial beings. He has the power of the home teaching program and priesthood quorums to see that the saving ordinances are extended to every ward member, as well as to deceased ancestors. Jacob and Joseph, the younger brothers of Nephi, as they were ordained teachers and priests among the people, gave us further light and knowledge:

> And we did magnify our office unto the Lord, taking upon us the responsibility, answering the sins of the people upon our own heads if we did not teach them the word of God with all diligence; wherefore, by laboring with our might their blood might not come upon our garments; otherwise their blood would come upon our garments, and we would not be found spotless at the last day. (Jacob 1:19)

The duties of the home teacher first of all include knowing the complete family in every way and gaining the love and respect of each member. Special interests, concerns, aspirations, schooling, church activity, birthdays, anniversaries, family interests, and professional careers are but a few areas that a home teacher should know about in order to gain respect and love from the family. After this confidence is gained, he should emphasize the importance of family and private prayers night and morning. Regular family home evenings, with all members of the family in attendance, should also be encouraged. Often, suggestions can be given as to how to make these evenings vital and important in the lives of each family member. Church activity, family history, missionary and temple work should be emphasized in the proper perspective. Above all, good gospel teaching should be brought into the home with each visit.

To convey the importance of the father and the patriarchal priesthood is one of the main goals of good home teaching. The father is the head of the family (regardless of Church membership), the priesthood leader, and the center focal point of the home.

Each home teacher should call upon the Lord for guidance, direction and inspiration in his home teaching assignments, both before calling on the homes and within the homes. On one occasion, two priests called upon their stake president as his home teachers. After arriving and making introductory comments, one of the priests asked: "Just what is the deal in this home teaching program, anyway? Do you, as stake president, really need home teachers?" The stake president answered with a definite "Yes!" He continued, "Let us kneel in prayer and see what the needs of this home are." After the prayer, one of the priests asked, "President, how is your family home evening program?" The president responded by saying, "Our prayers have been answered, brethren. This home needs to have the family home evening strengthened."

In order for the home teaching program to be completely successful, it is necessary that a personal priesthood interview (PPI) be held on a regular basis between the home teacher and the priesthood leader. This significant meeting will bring the ward resources and family needs together like no other link. Not only will it improve the performance of the home teacher, but it will bring the ward and the family closer together. Again, performance improves when measured, but performance improves remarkably when measured *and* reported. Home teaching is a revealed program for the Latter-day Saints. It can be one of the most rewarding experiences one can have in the Church.

WARD PRIESTHOOD EXECUTIVE COMMITTEE

The essential organization for administering to the needs of the Saints in the ward and in quorums, including the correlation of Melchizedek Priesthood and Aaronic Priesthood activity, is the ward priesthood executive committee. All priesthood leadership is represented in this significant committee. In addition to the bishopric, those in attendance should be the high priest group leader, ward mission leader, elders quorum president and Young Men's president, ward clerk, ward executive secretary, and others invited by the bishop. This select leadership is responsible for the spiritual growth in the ward.

The high priest group leader is responsible for the ward temple and family history programs. He should ask the following:

- How many temple recommend holders are there in the ward?
- How many could have recommends if appointments were made with the bishop?
- What do we need to do to prepare those who do not qualify?
- How many are attending the temple at least once a month?

- How many have completed the four-generation family group sheets?
- What do we need to do in order to complete this sacred task for all families?
- Is everyone preparing his or her own personal history?

The ward mission leader should ask the following:

- How many part-member families do we have?
- How can we engage each family member, especially the father, in the total ward program?
- What friendshipping programs do we need for potential ward members?
- How many baptisms have we had this year?
- Are all newly baptized members being completely friendshipped?

The elders quorum president represents all elders as well as all prospective elders. It is in the priesthood executive committee meeting that the president can utilize the total resources of the ward to bring all elders (or prospective elders) and their families into complete activity. Often, active children of partially active or prospective elders in the auxiliary and priesthood quorums are the source of conversion and activity in their own lives. The father of the home needs to believe the following:

- He is the head of his family;
- He does or can hold priesthood power to administer to all the needs of his family;
- The Church needs his service in many ways;
- The family will be improved by his activity; and
- He will be a better person for his activity.

The bishopric has responsibility for Aaronic Priesthood holders and young women of the same age. No young person should be neglected or forgotten. The youth programs bring vibrancy and spirit into the wards. Bishopric members should refer to their respective Church handbooks regarding responsibilities to the youth.

If every member of the ward priesthood executive committee functions as he should, the ward will become, in a sense, a "City of Enoch." Nothing less should be the goal.

WARD COUNCIL

The bishop presides over the ward council, just as he does the ward priesthood executive committee. In addition to members of the ward priesthood executive committee, the ward council also includes the Relief Society president, Sunday School president, Young Women's president, Primary president, the activities committee chairman, public communication director, and any others the bishop chooses to invite, such as the ward music chairman. There is a highly positive correlation between the success of this council and the complete spirituality of the ward.

Each quorum and ward organization is a separate part of the ward body, but related to it in some way. No one part of the council should feel it does not have need of the others. The ultimate principle is that quorums and organizations should work toward strengthening each other. Only with this attitude can the total ward body benefit from each part of the ward body. There should never be a feeling that one organization or quorum is more important or significant than another. The attitude should be one of "How can we serve each other in order to improve and enhance the total ward?"

FAMILY HOME EVENING

One of the most challenging yet most rewarding programs in the Church is family home evening. The fundamental purpose of mortality is to create and shape eternal family units. The priesthood kingdom of the family is the most significant organization in mortality and the only one that will exist eternally. Those experiences in mortality that create eternal family ties will bring true joy. On the contrary, any experiences that bring destruction to the eternal nature of the family will bring sorrow.

Within the home is where the most significant attitudes, appreciations, feelings, testimonies and eternal principles of living are taught and learned. Regularly held family home evenings, regardless of the nature of the activities, should be a strength to each family member. This powerful program will require the most demanding attention, planning, time and energy in order to be the most fruitful. Those homes which fulfill the purposes of family home evening will be blessed so that none of the family will be lost.

The leadership of the ward, including priesthood quorums, bishoprics, ward priesthood executive committees, ward councils, auxiliaries (and all other organizations) should place high priority on emphasizing family home evenings by providing instruction, planning, material, models and catalytic motivation. If all families are working toward the glory that comes from family home evenings, the wards and stakes of the Church will be blessed. Often, families struggle with lack of direction, insight, time and devotion to this vitally important revealed and divine program. Instructions from General Authorities are neglected. Manuals and resources are often overlooked. However, through prayer, effort and proper planning, every home can receive the blessings of family home evening to the extent that there will be joy and rejoicing in the immediate family and also in its posterity. When the family functions as it should, there is less need for the many programs of the Church.

Leaders in the wards and stake who place a major emphasis on family home evenings and effective home teaching will have given proper perspective to the most important activities in mortality. Those who do not emphasize these programs will suffer proportionately. Nothing will be able to compensate for failure in either program.

GOSPEL-ORIENTED TEACHING

One of the major endeavors of a ward should be to develop and call qualified and inspiring gospel-oriented teachers. The Lord has told us:

> Teach ye diligently and my grace shall attend you, that you may be instructed more perfectly in theory, in principle, in doctrine, in the law of the gospel, in all things that pertain unto the Kingdom of God, that are expedient for you to understand. (D&C 88:77-78)

Often, priesthood leaders neglect the importance of calling only the most qualified teachers. There is a compelling need for pre-service and in-service teacher training programs for all ward classes and at every level, from the earliest experiences of a child in the nursery to the oldest in quorums and gospel doctrine classes. The teacher should become anxiously engaged in teaching principles of the gospel at all times.

TRAITS OF A GOOD GOSPEL TEACHER

Perhaps the following traits could serve as a basis for teachers who continually strive to produce inspiring and stimulating lessons. A good gospel teacher should have:

A testimony as to the divine purpose of life.

This testimony should be so strong that the teacher does not get caught in the controversies of mankind. There must be a faith in God the Eternal Father, His Son Jesus Christ, the Holy Ghost, the restored gospel, the living prophet, the Book of Mormon, Doctrine and Covenants, and Pearl of Great Price. This faith is basic for continued and undeviating growth as a teacher of the Lord's gospel.

Love for the gospel.

The teacher who wants success and growth must know the gospel now and forever, keep the commandments to be entitled to His spirit, and live righteously. The soul of man is enriched by thinking, feeling and acting in harmony with truth. The Church needs teachers who, with sincere conviction and unflinching courage, will defend the gospel and declare it to an unbelieving world.

Love for teaching.

Developing a desire to share with others and observing the transformation of immature ideas into excellence are the experiences of a good teacher. A teacher's concept of his or her calling must be one of acceptance of a mission to develop strong testimonies of the divine gospel plan. Teachers should enjoy this work.

Ability to understand and enjoy people.

Without this attribute, teachers cannot extend their abilities of unlocking the hidden qualities that every person possesses. The student must experience a teacher who will listen, understand, and be concerned with his or her problems, which may not always pertain to gospel subjects.

Sincerity, humility and devotion to service.

A teacher's importance should never be of first consideration. Pride has no place in individual growth. The greatest happiness and satisfaction are derived from unselfish service with time and talents. This kind of service results in a complementary cycle. Humility is the solid foundation of all virtues. An important question we can ask a man is whether he be genuine or not. Is he authentic? Does he ring true? It is a terrible thing to deceive. It shatters confidence and creates suspicion, disillusionment and cynicism in the person deceived.

An individual style of teaching.

Whether a teacher excels in such methods as lecture, discussion, Socratic questioning, group dynamics, or the like, he must develop a style of teaching that is most conducive to his gifts and personality. This style must be sought, and then it should be refined.

A teaching attitude.

To read, study, think, mingle with people, exchange ideas and write are some of the ways of developing a successful teaching attitude. A teacher must be active and exert as much interest as possible in his area of teaching, or he may stagnate. An extended detour and possible deterioration may occur if a deaf ear is turned to teaching development.

Ability to create a good teaching environment.

Students need a lot of motivation and stimulation for creativity. Ideas that class members possess may not sprout or blossom in an improper environment. Expensive modern facilities are not necessary. What is necessary are good gospel subjects, materials, elimination of distracting and conflicting elements, and plenty of time to think and act.

Evaluation by students, other teachers and self.

Evaluation is essential for continued progress. Constructive criticism should not be taken personally, and appreciation needs to be given to those giving it. This process should not be short term, but one that never ceases. The best evaluation may not be known until a student has had an opportunity to demonstrate, in his own living, the principles implanted by his teacher.

A sense of humor.

Class members need to feel at ease and as if they have some things in common with the teacher. The sixth sense, the sense of humor, can be extended at the proper time and will help bring both student and teacher to a more accepting and comfortable environment.

Dynamic and enthusiastic feelings.

Enthusiasm and conviction must be present in all teaching. Many times teachers are not aware of the routine and habitually non-stimulating nature of their teaching. Students must feel the freshness and zest of presentations and ideas to be enthusiastic themselves. This is a reciprocal proposition that must first be generated by the teacher. Then each student can give his or her own reinforcement.

GUIDE FOR INCREASING SPIRITUALITY

1. Importance of the home stressed to all families.
   a. A weekly gathering for home evenings, as outlined in the manual. (*Family Home Evening Resource Book*, Salt Lake City: The Church of Jesus Christ of Latter-day Saints, 1983)
   b. Regular family prayers twice each day.
   c. Blessings on the food at all meals.
   d. An emphasis on "The Golden Rule" within the home.
   e. Reading of the scriptures as a family group each day.
   f. Teaching of love at home, family harmony, fair play.
   g. Occasional family council meetings where rules and regulations of the home are considered and accepted by all. (These meetings help a great deal in avoiding unpleasantness later, especially in the children.)

2. Regular temple attendance (at least once a month) by the stake presidency, high council, Melchizedek Priesthood quorum presidencies, and the bishoprics.

3. A spirit of dedication on the part of officers and teachers, and on the part of members, a remembrance of their covenants with the Lord.

a. All live good LDS lives, both in and out of the home.

b. All accept assigned responsibilities and carry them through.

c. All obey the commandments:

1) Maintain LDS standards of conduct.

2) Pay full tithes.

3) Fast on fast day and pay generous offerings.

4) Obey the Word of Wisdom. Don't "cut corners" or make excuses.

5) Honor the Sabbath Day.

6) Respect Church leaders.

7) Avoid gossip and criticism.

8) Attend all meetings.

4. Good preparation on the part of executives and teachers.

a. Executives: Know your callings and study the handbooks.

b. Teachers: teach well prepared with a gospel-oriented approach.

c. Conduct meetings efficiently.

d. Be punctual in starting and ending meetings.

e. Follow the program outlined by the presiding brethren.

5. Quality in sacrament meetings and all other meetings.

a. Prepare programs that are both instructive and inspirational about gospel principles.

b. Maintain reverence.

6. Efficiency in home teaching.
   a. Quality.
   b. Quantity.
   c. Dedication (an essential element).

7. Temple marriage taught to the youth as doctrine.

8. Adequate recreation in the stake.
   a. An occasional social for the stake presidency and high council members and their wives.
   b. Semi-annual socials and programs for the stake presidency, high council, bishoprics, clerks and wives.
   c. Annual social and program for stake presidency, stake auxiliary boards, high council advisers, and husbands and wives of these members.
   d. Ward and stake activity programs for the youth.

9. Family history research program, which urges people to save their own dead, in addition to those provided for them when they attend the temple.

10. Current temple recommends for all eligible ward members, and temple attendance at least once a month. Goals set for those not eligible for temple blessings.

11. An effective youth program with regular and well conducted Aaronic Priesthood programs.

CHAPTER VII

ESTABLISHING PURPOSES, GOALS AND RESPONSIBILITIES...

Family Home Evening and Home Teaching

Family History and Temple Activities

Ward Family History Leaders

Priesthood Missionary Work

Priesthood Welfare Program

The Law of the Fast

Quorums

ESTABLISHING PURPOSES, GOALS AND RESPONSIBILITIES...

The stake presidency directs the Melchizedek Priesthood programs of the stake. The responsibility of high council advisers and quorum presidencies is to do everything possible to help each Melchizedek Priesthood bearer in the stake keep the oath and covenant made when he accepted the higher priesthood.

The five areas of priesthood responsibility and activity within the Church today are:

1. Family history and temple work
2. Welfare programs
3. Missionary service
4. Family home evening
5. Home teaching

The primary purpose of these five areas of priesthood activity is to provide for the spiritual and temporal well-being of every Church member and to bring about the purposes of the Lord in this dispensation. (See *Melchizedek Priesthood Leadership Handbook, 1990*)

FAMILY HOME EVENING AND HOME TEACHING

1. Purpose of programs
   a. The family home evening program is designed to
      give each ward and stake member a real-life, day-to-
      day living experience as the member of a family
      with appropriate responsibilities. All members
      should have an ideal environment where true gospel
      living is practiced and "seen in action." As a result of
      this experience, they should be better able to handle
      their roles as family members in the world today.
   b. The home is the *first* and *most effective* place for
      children to learn life's lessons, which are truth,
      honor, virtue, self-control, the value of education,
      honest work, and the purpose and privilege of life.
      Nothing can take the place of home in rearing and
      teaching children, and "no other success can
      compensate for failure in the home" (David O.
      McKay). The purpose of the home teaching
      program is to implement the Lord's instructions that
      priesthood members are to visit the homes of each
      member, exhorting families "to pray vocally and in
      secret and attend to all family duties" (D&C 20:51)
      The Lord instructs the priesthood also "to watch

over the Church always, and be with and strengthen them" (D&C 20:53).

Home teaching isn't just one of the programs...it is the instrument by which we see to it, through the priesthood, that every program in the Church is made available to parents and their children. In watching over the families assigned to them, home teachers represent the bishop in ward responsibilities and the quorum leaders in priesthood responsibilities.

2. Goals

a. To implement family home evening and home teaching programs in the wards, as directed by the General Authorities of the Church, following the guidelines and instructions outlined in Church handbooks and other publications.

b. To provide the vital link between the priesthood member and his quorum, and between his family and the ward. The home teacher provides this by bringing the needs of the family into contact with the needs of the quorum, of the ward and of the entire Church.

c. To develop in each ward member a sense of responsibility and concern for himself and his fellowman. To teach him self-control, humility, and a willingness to curb desires for the good of another.

d. To help build an active testimony of the restored gospel in each individual so that all will have a greater appreciation for, and a more solid commitment to, the Church and family life.

e. To provide an opportunity for each ward member to join in a congenial, relaxed and informal setting where the gospel can truly be practiced and seen in action. To promote loyalty, respect, love, devotion, appreciation and responsibility one for another in each family.

f. To insure that all ward members know the organization of the Church, its programs, its offerings and its sincere concern for each as individuals and as family members.

g. To increase spirituality among ward members by fasting and praying together, attending church together, studying together, playing together, and growing together.

h. To encourage participation in church activities and social affairs that will aid in the spiritual, cultural and social education of individuals.

i. To give each ward member the opportunity to demonstrate love for others in a natural family setting and to be loved and appreciated in return.

j. To help each ward member know and realize that he
or she is an important and necessary person. To
have members feel they are worthwhile to
themselves and to others.

k. To emphasize the importance of the home and of
teaching the gospel within it. To show each member
that the home is truly the basis of a righteous and
good life, that no other instrumentality can take its
place, that the home is the family castle, a sanctuary
where peace and rest are found, where love and
affection abound, and where the cares of the world
are left outside.

3. Program Responsibilities

a. Bishopric: The coordination of these programs on a
ward basis is the responsibility of the bishopric. It is
the bishopric's priesthood duty to develop, organize,
and put into effect successful programs in all areas
with the assistance of the quorum presidencies.
Appropriate priesthood executive committee and
ward council meetings should be held weekly and
monthly under the direction of the bishopric. Reports
should be received each week from the quorum
presidencies, and interviews should be conducted
with each of these brethren. The bishopric should

submit appropriate reports to the stake presidency before the end of each month.

b. Executive Secretary: It is suggested that the executive secretary generally follow the duties outlined for him in the priesthood manuals and that he be given similar duties in the family home evening program.

c. Quorum Presidencies: These brethren, under the direction of the bishopric, have the responsibility to supervise and put into effect the home teaching and family home evening programs. Each can have responsibility for his portion of the ward: the families and the home teachers. On a weekly basis, appropriate oral and written reports should be passed from the family heads to home teachers, who in turn pass them to the quorum presidencies, who give them to the bishopric. Each member of the quorum presidencies should accomplish the following:

1) Coordinate with the bishopric in calling home teachers.

2) Supervise, motivate, and provide training for home teachers under his leadership.

3) Help his home teachers realize the responsibility they have for others.

4) Challenge home teachers with appropriate tasks pertaining to their assigned families.

5) Encourage home teachers to visit their families frequently (at least once a month) and to visit individual family members as needed.

6) Receive oral and written reports from the home teachers on a weekly basis and conduct a formal interview each month.

7) Give oral and written reports to the bishopric on a weekly basis and a formal oral evaluation once a month.

d. Home Teachers: Each pair of home teachers has responsibility for its assigned families. In approaching his assignment, a home teacher should always remember that he serves his families in much the same way the bishop serves the ward. A home teacher can have much more than a message to give or a visit to make. Through love, selfless service, example and teaching, he should aim to build spirituality in each individual and to help each family walk uprightly before the Lord and find joy and satisfaction in living the gospel. A home teacher will likely find that more than one visit a month will be necessary in order to fully discharge his responsibility to a family. The following suggestions are offered for home teachers:

1) Make friends with your families. The Prophet Joseph Smith once asked, "Whom can I teach

but my friends?" Before a home teacher can be effective, he must win the friendship and respect of his families.

2) Show genuine interest in each family member. Learn the names of every individual and call each by name.

3) Plan your visits. Home teaching partners should meet together and prepare before making their visits.

4) Make an appointment with each family, or establish a standard time on a particular evening so that you will be expected. (Make your initial monthly visit during the first week of each month.) Don't just "pop in" at some unexpected moment. Strive to avoid interrupting favorite television programs or other family activities.

5) Plan short, meaningful visits to each family. Usually fifteen to twenty minutes in length is sufficient, although more time may be needed for the initial visit each month. Always remember that you are a guest in the home.

6) Plan to assist the family in every way that you can, always recognizing the father, if there is one, as the authority figure in the home.

7) Observe attitudes and activities of each member of the family.

8) Make all gospel discussions meaningful. If a gospel message is to be presented, have it well thought out. Both home teachers and family members should be encouraged to participate in the discussions.

9) Invite suggestions from the family. An effective home teacher is a good listener. Remember that the father of the home, if there is one, is the patriarch and it is he who presides.

10) Go the second mile with your family. Home teaching restricted to only monthly visits cannot be fully successful.

11) Provide families with Church activities information, attend special family events (like baptisms), recognize birthdays, inquire about family members away from home, and help arrange transportation when needed.

12) Meet all deadlines when reporting to your priesthood leader each month. Seek his advice.

4. Policies and Procedures

a. Home Teaching Interview: The oral evaluation provides a system for transmitting pertinent information concerning families and family members to the proper authority. Interviews are made by the senior home teacher to the quorum

presidency, and in turn to the bishopric and the stake
president. Particular needs and problems of those
concerned are discussed; possible solutions are
considered and positive corrective action is taken at
the lowest practical level of authority. However,
these things can and should be taken to the highest
authority necessary to secure satisfactory solutions.
Intimate personal problems and strictly confidential
information should be referred directly to the bishop.

b. Home Teachers: The bishopric, the quorum
presidency and the general secretary of the Aaronic
Priesthood are responsible for choosing, calling and
assigning home teachers in each ward. When
assigning home teachers to families, these groups
should consider the number of families in the ward
and the needs of each. Special problems should be
met with special teachers; particularly wise and
tactful home teachers should be assigned where
home teachers may not be welcome.

Generally speaking, all priesthood members in the
ward should be called as home teachers, with senior
home teaching roles being given to Melchizedek
Priesthood holders, and junior companion roles
being given to Aaronic Priesthood holders. The use
of all priesthood bearers in the ward provides
strength for the home teaching program. Exceptions

are made for members of stake presidencies, high councils and bishoprics, who are generally not given home teaching assignments.

After the bishop and Melchizedek and Aaronic priesthood leaders have determined which home teachers to call and which families they should visit, each home teacher should be called in for a private interview. During this interview, the home teacher should be asked if he is willing to accept complete responsibility for this assignment, as well as for his own attendance at all ward meetings.

FAMILY HISTORY AND TEMPLE ACTIVITIES

1. Objectives
   a. To bring into proper perspective the fourth correlation principle (family history and temple work), which incorporates principles for our exaltation as well as for those who have passed on.
   b. To prepare the members of the stake for future leadership in Church family history and temple activities.
   c. To provide incentives for individuals to do family history and temple work.

2. Goals
   a. To encourage each endowed member to attend temple sessions on a regular basis.
   b. To give the youth opportunities to attend ward baptismal excursions.
   c. To encourage each member, single or married, to submit the family group sheets requested in the priesthood three- and four-generation programs.
   d. To assist individuals in original research and temple work for their families.
   e. To motivate members to write personal and family histories.

f. To encourage members, when called, to participate in the record extraction programs.

3. Suggestions for Implementing this Program:
   a. Launch programs in each ward (through motivational talks by the bishop and other individuals in leadership positions).
   b. Formulate time-scheduled family history programs (where ward members work toward a goal of submitting at least one family group sheet by a set date).
   c. Plan ward temple excursions. (Make them important!)
   d. Enlist adult members in priesthood family history workshops (at least one six-week workshop for each adult).

4. Quorum Presidency Family History Responsibilities
   In addition to assisting and advising the bishop in overall family history matters, the quorum presidency has the following duties:
   a. Help direct ward temple excursions.
   b. Direct priesthood family history workshops.
   c. With the help of the home teacher, follow up on family history assignments.
   d. Encourage members to complete their assignments in the four-generation family group sheet program.

e. Organize ward record examiners and direct the ward
   record examining program.
f. Submit, under the quorum presidency's direction, a
   ward family history report. This report should
   include the following:
   1) Number of temple endowments (for both men
      and women).
   2) Number of baptisms for the dead.
   3) Number of *twice* initialed family group sheets
      (four-generation program).
   4) Number of large individual-entry forms
      submitted.
   5) Completion of individual and family histories.
g. Perform other responsibilities as outlined in the
   Church Family History Instructions.

5. Instructional Program for Family History
   A workshop for ward examiners, specialists, family
history teachers and priesthood advisers should be held
each Sunday during the usual class period for Sunday
School.

WARD FAMILY HISTORY LEADERS

1. Family History Coordinator
   a. Supervise family history and temple activities in the ward, under the direction of the bishop.
   b. With the bishopric, set family history objectives and see that they are carried out.
   c. Become acquainted with other ward programs; use those that will improve programs you are conducting.

2. Endowment Coordinator
   a. Maintain a record of all endowed people in the ward.
   b. Inform endowed ward members of temple excursions and invite them to attend.
   c. Collect bus fare for those assigned to attend temple excursions.
   d. Keep a record of all completed ward endowments.
   e. Report information monthly to the ward clerk.

3. Transportation Coordinator
   a. Arrange for a bus to be used for ward temple excursions.
   b. Arrange for lunches or refreshments if these are desired.

4. Baptismal Coordinator
   a. Follow up after the bishop's interviews to make sure that all interviewed persons get on the bus.
   b. Collect transportation fees for baptismal excursions.

5. Instructor
   a. Learn from ward leaders what goals have been set for the ward.
   b. Prepare lessons thoroughly, keeping in mind these ward goals.
   c. Meet family history goals expected of each ward member.
   d. Become personally acquainted with each member of the class.
   e. Attend all meetings called to integrate and improve family history in the ward.

6. Examiners
   a. Examine group sheets.
   b. Recommend necessary corrections.
   c. Return group sheets to the individuals who submitted them.
   d. Submit sheets needing no correction to family history coordinator.

7. Typists

Assist in typing corrected group sheets in preparation for their submission to the stake.

PRIESTHOOD MISSIONARY WORK

1. Bishops
   a. Call "missionary-minded" home teachers to visit part-member and nonmember families or individuals.
   b. Attend baptisms of new members. Give them the first friendshipping lesson shortly after baptism, in cooperation with home teachers and stake missionaries.
   c. Recommend names of prospective stake missionaries to the high council representative of the ward. (High councilors should also recommend names.) These should be members who know the missionary discussions and who are sufficiently free of military reserve training programs, heavy work loads, and employment obligations so as to be able to devote part of Saturday and all day Sunday to missionary activities. First consideration should be given to recommending qualified priesthood holders for missionary service.
   d. Invite a ward member serving as a stake missionary to be a member of the ward priesthood executive committee.

2. Home Teachers

    a. Introduce nonmembers to missionaries early on and work toward nonmember attendance at Sunday School, firesides and cottage meetings. If possible, accompany them to such functions.

    b. Pave the way for, but do not present, missionary lessons through home teaching.

    c. Following baptisms, cooperate with the bishop and teacher in presenting six friendshipping lessons to new members.

    d. Meet frequently with stake missionaries concerning nonmembers.

    e. Attend workshops and other meetings scheduled by the stake mission presidency.

3. Quorum Presidents and Group Leaders

    a. Place missionary business on the meeting agendas of quorum presidency, quorum, and ward priesthood executive committee meetings, along with the other three phases of priesthood correlation.

    b. See that quorum members are spiritually and intellectually prepared to carry missionary callings as the Church may require.

    c. Schedule time at quorum meetings for stake missionaries to briefly request, as they deem necessary, the assistance of the quorum or individuals in seeking out contacts, developing contacts with investigators, teaching and friendshipping investigators, or assisting converts in their growth in the Melchizedek Priesthood.

d. In response to requests from the stake mission president, call upon members of the quorum to supplement efforts of stake missionaries in prebaptismal friendshipping and other missionary-related activities.

e. Maintain quorum contact with the ward's full-time missionaries serving in the field.

f. Hear reports from return missionaries on the progress of their missions, on new missionary procedures, and on their personal successes.

g. Friendship return missionaries, integrating them into the quorum and helping them adjust to school and work.

h. Encourage financial support of and participation in family-to-family Book of Mormon programs.

i. Familiarize the quorum with new missionary tools and friendshipping materials as they become available, e.g., filmstrips, tapes, and motion pictures.

4. Missionaries

a. Consult frequently with the home teachers assigned to visit nonmember and part-member families. Give

aid, advice, and counsel to them as they carry out
their assigned duties.

b. Serve on the ward priesthood executive committee as
called upon by the bishop.

c. Teach lessons to nonmembers.

d. Work closely with full-time missionaries.

PRIESTHOOD WELFARE PROGRAM

The objective of the welfare program is to help ward members value the fundamental principles of work, thrift, dignity, and self-reliance so that they may apply these principles fully to their lives and eradicate all tendencies toward idleness, unnecessary debt and waste. The program should also emphasize the significance of the family unit so that priesthood bearers and heads of households are encouraged to guide the activities of their homes and apply the correct principles of Church welfare. Some of these principles are:

- Storing in anticipation of need.
- Being thrifty and industrious.
- Caring for one's own.
- Preparing for the future.
- Giving of self and of means to the Church welfare program and the community.

From time to time during the year, each quorum should be supplied with details concerning the following, so that these goals might be realized.

All families should begin a program of storing a year's supply of food, clothing, and if possible, fuel.

Each person and family should learn principles of thrift and industry and of avoiding unnecessary debt.

Each person should prepare himself to care for his or her own needs and for those of family members and relatives who might be physically, socially or emotionally unable to provide for themselves.

Each person should prepare for the future by becoming trained to work in some gainful employment.

Each person should learn and observe the law of the fast.

LAW OF THE FAST

Every member of the stake should understand the law of the fast and observe it faithfully.

1. Bishops are to acquaint members of their wards with the program by holding a special sacrament meeting on the law of the fast and then reporting the results.

2. Priesthood leaders, through home teaching, are to help families understand the law of the fast and report the effectiveness of their teaching.

3. Minimum fast offering goal: the equivalent cost of two meals.

4. Recommended time for collection of fast offerings: on Fast Sunday, before completion of the Sunday meal.

QUORUMS

The following is a brief description of the duties and responsibilities of quorum presidencies. These are merely guidelines to assist presidencies in accomplishing a job well done.

The president or group leader of a quorum is given his calling by the stake presidency. He holds the keys to administering to the needs of his quorum members. He selects his counselors through approval from the stake presidency.

Members of the quorum presidency have the responsibility to be examples to their quorum members. They should maintain relationships of respect and love with each member. These personal relationships encourage members to accept assignments and challenges with positive action.

The following are suggestions for carrying out assignments:

1. Delegate jobs and assignments to all members of the quorum.

2. Make sure you understand and support all ward programs.

3. Be positive in your approach. Be demanding but not "pushy." Let the quorum know that assignments should be completed promptly for the Lord, not for you.

4. Plan several socials during the year for your quorum. For example, attend games or go to the temple together.

5. Hold weekly presidency meetings to discuss assignments, problems, etc.

6. Interview every member of the quorum as soon as possible.

7. Give the bishopric full support in the programs of the ward. Keep the bishop and his counselors informed of all your activities.

8. Maintain good communication between your quorum and the bishopric, stake presidency, and high councilor.

9. Have a friendshipping committee in your quorum.

10. Involve everyone in projects, activities, home teaching, and family history.

11. Give every quorum member a challenge.

12. Keep up good communications between the presidency and quorum members.

CHAPTER VIII

...WILL PERFECT AND SANCTIFY THE SAINTS.

Perfecting

Proclaiming

Redeeming

DALE MORTIMER

...WILL PERFECT AND SANCTIFY THE SAINTS.

Our Heavenly Father has an unequivocal, eternal and exalting love for each of His children. It is difficult for us, with our mortal understanding, to comprehend the depth of this immortal love. Each of us has been blessed with a mortal body as a result of the unselfish sacrifices of Adam and Eve. Through the indescribable atoning sacrifice of the Savior, the bonds of death have been broken so that each of us has the privilege to be resurrected and the opportunity to return to the presence of Jesus Christ and God the Father with our worthy families. The priesthood and Church of God have been restored with all of their sacred and eternal ordinances and with a living prophet who serves as the Lord's mouthpiece on earth. The Church of Jesus Christ has established, through revelation, priesthood programs that will inspire and enable families to be sealed together forever.

PERFECTING

Souls are all so individual because of differences in personality, testimony, experience, talent, desire, aspiration, confidence, understanding, worthiness, etc. Even with all these differences, everyone is precious in the sight of the Lord. Because of such diversity among souls, the Church must have flexibility and inspiration in administering its programs. "For the letter [of the law] killeth, but the spirit [of the law] giveth life" (2 Cor. 3:6).

Every leader must understand that the ultimate personal goals for effective leadership are "faith, hope, charity and love, with an eye single to the glory of God" (D&C 4:5). There should be no limitations, obstructions or discouragements in reaching each of our brothers and sisters.

The home can be the ultimate setting for developing eternal understandings, testimonies of the divinity of Christ and His church, righteousness, love, worthiness, desire and other qualities of godliness that qualify each family member to return to the presence of our Heavenly Father. In the eternities to come, there will be no need for the Church organization and programs, because the patriarchal order of the family will reign. For these significant reasons, quality family home evening and home teaching programs are supreme goals for each of us.

PROCLAIMING

As the Saints become more perfected, so should they also become more involved in proclaiming the gospel of Jesus Christ. Each person should learn to "open his mouth" and make a golden friend by presenting some unique principle of the gospel that could spark an interest and result in a missionary referral. This is but one way to proclaim the divine gospel message.

All members should have a desire to invite nonmembers and full-time missionaries to cottage meetings or family home evenings. On these occasions, the missionaries may present films like *Man's Search for Happiness* or *Together Forever.* These experiences can prepare the way for visits to nonmembers' homes, where additional films may be shown, such as *The First Vision* or *The Priesthood Restored,* and further discussions may be given, both of which may lead to baptism. Every member should become involved in the family-to-family Book of Mormon project, in which individuals or families enclose personal testimonies and pictures in gift copies of the Book of Mormon.

Every family within the Church should make it a goal to prepare a way for each young man (and each young woman who so desires) to become a full-time missionary. Also, after children are grown, fathers and mothers should visit with their bishops regarding full-time missions of their own.

REDEEMING

From early childhood, family members should learn the importance of temple marriage and strive for this goal. Family histories, pedigree charts and family group sheets should be prepared and submitted to the Church Family History files and then sent to temples for exalting ordinances. Through regular temple attendance, members have the opportunity to renew all sacred covenants made in priesthood ordinances, thus bringing inspiration, revelation, direction and commitment into their lives. Living lives worthy of temple recommends and fulfilling all of the sacred covenants made in the House of the Lord will not only help prepare each member for exaltation but will bring immeasurable joy to souls in the spirit world anxiously pleading for this sacred work to be performed. The gospel of Abraham, our gospel, is celestial marriage. (D&C 110:12)

When we serve the Lord and participate in all of the temple blessings (worthiness being our goal), we will receive blessings beyond mortal comprehension. Each of us will have the power to come forth in the first resurrection, inheriting kingdoms, thrones, principalities, powers, dominions, and all heights and depths (D&C 132:19). Saints who gain such rewards shall "pass by the angels, and the gods, which are set there, to their exaltation and glory in all things, as hath been sealed upon their heads, which glory shall be a fulness and a continuation of the seeds forever and ever" (D&C 132:19). We must realize we share in the promises Abraham received "concerning his seed, and of the fruit of his loins...that they should continue as innumerable as the stars; or, if ye were to count the sand upon the seashore ye could not number them" (D&C 132:30).

Yes, brethren, the rewards far exceed the inconveniences and challenges given us as priesthood leaders. If only we completely understood who we are and what eternal blessings lie in store for each of us and our families, God's work would roll forth with unconquerable faith and undeniable results. The Lord Himself has said in a dramatic way:

> Brethren, shall we not go on in so great a cause?...Courage, brethren; and on, on to the victory! Let your hearts rejoice, and be exceedingly glad. Let the earth break forth into singing. Let the dead speak forth anthems of eternal praise to the King Immanuel, who hath ordained, before the world was, that which would enable us to redeem them out of their prison; for the prisoners shall go free. (D&C 128:22)

Then within our hearts there will be joy bursting forth, for the Savior has said:

Let the mountains shout for joy, and all ye valleys cry aloud; and all ye seas and dry lands tell the wonders of your Eternal King! And ye rivers, and brooks, and rills, flow down with gladness. Let the woods and all the trees of the field praise the Lord; and ye solid rocks weep for joy! And let the sun, moon and the morning stars sing together and let all the sons of God shout for joy! And let the eternal creations declare his name forever and ever! And again I say, how glorious is the voice we hear from heaven, proclaiming in our ears, glory, and salvation, and honor, and immortality, and eternal life; kingdoms, principalities, and powers! (D&C 128:23)

INDEX

Temple ix, 11, 42, 83, 85, 87, 89, 100, 102–3, 105, 107, 118–21, 132, 140
Temple blessings 103, 140
Temporal 18, 26, 30, 107
Testimony 28, 96, 110, 136
Theories 13
Thrifty 128
Time x, 3, 6, 8, 18, 25, 27, 33, 37, 45–46, 66, 76–79, 93–94, 97–99, 114, 119, 125, 130
Tithing 83
Traits 21–22, 81, 96
Transgress 44
True 13, 15–16, 21, 71, 93, 97, 108
Truth 3, 14, 30–31, 33, 96, 108

U

Unrighteous 10
Unselfish 19, 26, 97, 135
Unveil x, 33

V

Valiant x, 23
Value 26, 32, 70, 75, 108, 128
Verbal symbolism 57
Virtue 31, 33, 97, 108
Volunteer 38, 41

W

Ward 3, 5–10, 38–42, 44, 54, 69, 74–76, 81, 83, 85–86, 88–95, 102–3, 105, 108–13, 116–22, 124–28, 130–32
Ward council 5, 81, 83, 92–93, 111
Ward mission leader 89–90
Ward music chairman 92
Watchman 85
Weakness 9, 70, 80
Welfare 85, 105, 107, 128
Whole person 74
Wicked 13, 32, 47, 85
Wickedness 30, 85
Wife 40

Wisdom 7, 21, 26
Wise 18, 45, 55, 58, 65, 116
Word of Wisdom 101
Work 124–25
Workshop 119–20, 125
World 3, 11–12, 14, 29–30, 96, 108, 111, 141
Worth 9, 12, 16
Worthiness 38, 40, 43–44, 136, 140
Worthy 17, 45, 135, 140

Y

Young Men's president 89
Young women 91
Young Women's president 92
Youth 91, 102, 118
Youth program 41, 91, 103

Z

Zion 38